C Programming Practice

By PRASUN BARUA

TABLE OF CONTENTS

CHAPTER NO.	TITLE	PAGE NO.
INTRODUCTION	INTRODUCTION	5
CHAPTER-1:	WHAT IS C PROGRAMMING?	6
CHAPTER-2:	WHY C PROGRAMMING?	7
CHAPTER-3:	APPLICATIONS OF C PROGRAMMING	8
CHAPTER-4:	C BASIC COMMANDS	9
CHAPTER-5:	HOW C PROGRAMMING LANGUAGE WORKS?	10
CHAPTER-6:	Hello World Program in C	11
CHAPTER-7:	Printing Number Entered by User	12
CHAPTER-8:	Adding Two Numbers	13
CHAPTER-9:	Finding Quotient and Remainder	14
CHAPTER-10:	Finding Size of int, float, double and char in Your System	15
CHAPTER-11:	Swapping Two Numbers	16
CHAPTER-12:	Finding ASCII Value of a Character	18
CHAPTER-13:	Multiplying two Numbers	19
CHAPTER-14:	Finding Area and Circumference of Circle	20
CHAPTER-15:	Converting a person's name in Abbreviated	21
CHAPTER-16:	Calculating A Simple Interest	22
CHAPTER-17:	Finding the Largest Number Among Three Numbers	23
CHAPTER-18:	Finding The Gross Salary of an Employee	24
CHAPTER-19:	Calculating Percentage of 5 Subjects	25
CHAPTER-20:	Converting Temperature Celsius into Fahrenheit	26
CHAPTER-21:	Finding out the size of the different data types in C	27
CHAPTER-22:	Checking Whether a Number is Positive or Negative	28
CHAPTER-23:	Checking whether a character is a vowel or not	29

CHAPTER NO.	TITLE	PAGE NO.
CHAPTER-24:	Calculating Factorial of a Number	30
CHAPTER-25:	Reading Integer (N) and Printing First Three Powers (N^1,N^2,N^3)	31
CHAPTER-26:	Swapping two numbers without third variable	32
CHAPTER-27:	Printing Address of Variable	33
CHAPTER-28:	Checking Whether a Number is Even or Odd	34
CHAPTER-29:	Checking whether an Alphabet is Vowel or Consonant	35
CHAPTER-30:	Finding the Largest Number Among Three Numbers	36
CHAPTER-31:	FINDING THE ROOTS OF A QUADRATIC EQUATION	37
CHAPTER-32:	Calculating the Sum of Natural Numbers	39
CHAPTER-33:	Checking Leap Year	40
CHAPTER-34:	Factorial Program using recursion in C	42
CHAPTER-35:	Generating Multiplication Table	43
CHAPTER-36:	Fibonacci Series using recursion in C	44
CHAPTER-37:	Finding GCD of two Numbers	45
CHAPTER-38:	Finding LCM of two Numbers	46
CHAPTER-39:	Reversing a Number	47
CHAPTER-40:	Calculating the Power of a Number	48
CHAPTER-41:	Checking Whether a Number is Palindrome or Not	49
CHAPTER-	Checking Whether a Number is Prime or Not	50

CHAPTER NO.	TITLE	PAGE NO.
CHAPTER-43:	Displaying Prime Numbers Between Two Intervals	51
CHAPTER-44:	Checking Armstrong Number	52
CHAPTER-45:	Displaying Armstrong Number Between Two Intervals	54
CHAPTER-46:	Finding Factors of a Number	56
CHAPTER-47:	Making a Simple Calculator to Add, Subtract, Multiply or Divide Using switch…case	58
CHAPTER-48:	Printing A Message Multiple Times Using Loop	60
CHAPTER-49:	Printing Truth Table of XY+Z Using Loop	61
CHAPTER-50:	Converting Decimal Number to Binary Number Using Loop	63
CHAPTER-51:	Swapping Two Numbers Using Functions	65
CHAPTER-52:	Checking Prime Number by Creating a Function	67
CHAPTER-53:	Calculating Factorial of a Number Using Recursion	69
CHAPTER-54:	Finding Fibonacci Series Using Functions	70
CHAPTER-55:	Performing All Arithmetic Operations Using Functions	72
CHAPTER-56:	Calculating Power Using Recursion	75
CHAPTER-57:	Converting Binary Number to Decimal and vice-versa	77
CHAPTER-58:	Converting Octal Number to Decimal and vice-versa	79
CHAPTER-59:	Converting Binary Number to Octal and vice-versa	81
CHAPTER-60:	Converting A Lower Case To Upper Case using string	84
CHAPTER-61:	Calculating Average of Numbers Using Arrays	85

CHAPTER-62:	Finding The Length Of Any String	86
CHAPTER-63:	Checking Number Is Even Or Odd Using If/Else Statements	87
CHAPTER-64:	Checking Year Is Leap Year Or Not Using If/Else Statements	88
CHAPTER-65:	Finding Max Number Among Given Three Number Using If/Else Statements	90
CHAPTER-66:	Finding Quotient And Reminder Of Two Numbers Using If/Else Statements	92
CHAPTER-67:	Temperature Conversion Celsius To Fahrenheit And Vice Versa Using Switch Case	94
CHAPTER-68:	Calculating Area Of Circle Rectangle And Triangle Using Switch Case	96
CHAPTER-69:	Reading Infinite Number Then Arrange Ascending Order Using Pointer	100
CHAPTER-70:	Storing Information of a Student in a Structure	103
CHAPTER-71:	Calculating Difference Between Two Time Period	106

INTRODUCTION

Welcome to the "C Programming Practice"! This book contains various topics and exercises on c programming. Before proceeding with these exercises, you should have a basic understanding of C Programming language terminologies. A basic understanding of C programming language will assist you in understanding the programming concepts and move fast on the learning track. It will be great pleasure if this book helps you to know about C programming. Thanks for reading the book.

CHAPTER-1: WHAT IS C PROGRAMMING?

C is a general-purpose programming language which is one of the popular, simple and basic program. It is a structured programming language which is machine-independent and extensively used to write various applications. For example, we can say about Operating System Windows and many other complex programs such as Oracle database, Git, Python interpreter, and more. It is flexible to use.

A great computer scientist Dennis Ritchie created a new programming language called 'C' at the Bell Laboratories in 1972. It was created from 'ALGOL', 'BCPL' and 'B' programming languages. 'C' programming language contains all the features of these languages and many more additional concepts that make it unique from other languages.

'C' is a powerful programming language related to the UNIX operating system. Most of the UNIX operating system is coded in 'C'. In the past, 'C' programming was limited to the UNIX operating system. Due to rapid growth of it around the world, it became commercial, and many compilers were released for cross-platform systems. Nowadays, 'C' runs under a variety of operating systems and hardware platforms. In 1989, American National Standards Institute (ANSI) defined a commercial standard for 'C' language for maintaining the standard of 'C' language. In 1990, International Standards Organization (ISO) approved it. 'C' programming language is also known as 'ANSI C'.

CHAPTER-2: WHY C PROGRAMMING?

'C' is a base language for many programming languages. So, learning 'C' as the main language will play an important role while studying other programming languages. It shares the same concepts such as data types, operators, control statements and many more. 'C' can be used widely in various applications. It is a simple language which provides faster execution. There are many jobs available for a 'C' developer in the current market.

'C' is a structured programming language which is distinguished into various modules. Each module can be written distinctly and together it forms a single 'C' program. This structure makes it easy for testing, maintaining and debugging processes. 'C' contains 32 keywords, various data types and a set of powerful built-in functions that make programming very efficient.

A 'C' program contains various functions which are part of a library. It can outspread itself. We can add our features and functions to the library. We can access and use these functions anytime we want in our program. This feature makes it simple while working with complex programming. Various compilers are available in the market that can be used for executing programs written in this language.

'C' is a vastly portable language. It can run on other machines. This feature helps users to use or execute the code on another computer.

CHAPTER-3: APPPLICATIONS OF C PROGRAMMING

- 'C' is widely used for developing desktop applications.
- Most of the applications by Adobe are developed using 'C' programming language.
- 'C' language is widely used in embedded systems as well as compiler production.
- It is used for developing system and IOT applications.
- 'C' is used for developing browsers and their extensions. Google's Chromium is built using 'C' programming language.
- For developing databases 'C' is used. MySQL is the most popular database software which is built using 'C'.
- It is used in developing an operating system. Operating systems like Apple's OS X, Microsoft's Windows, and Symbian are developed using 'C' language. It is used for developing desktop and mobile phone's operating system.

CHAPTER-4: C BASIC COMMANDS

Some basic commands of C programming language are as follows:

C Basic commands	Explanation
#include <stdio.h>	This command comprises standard input output header file(stdio.h) from the C library before compiling a C program
int main()	This is the main function from where C program execution begins.
{	It indicates the beginning of the main function.
/*_some_comments_*/	Whatever written inside this command "/* */" inside a C program, it will not be considered for compilation and execution.
printf("Hello_World! ");	This command prints the output on the screen.
getch();	This command is used for any character input from keyboard.
return 0;	For terminating a C program (main function, thus command is used. It returns 0.
}	It indicates the end of the main function.

CHAPTER-5: HOW C PROGRAMMING LANGUAGE WORKS?

C is basically a compiled language which uses a special tool called compiler. The compiler compiles the program and converts it into the object file which is machine readable. After the compilation process, the linker will combine different object files and creates a single executable file to run the program. The execution of a 'C' program as below diagram:

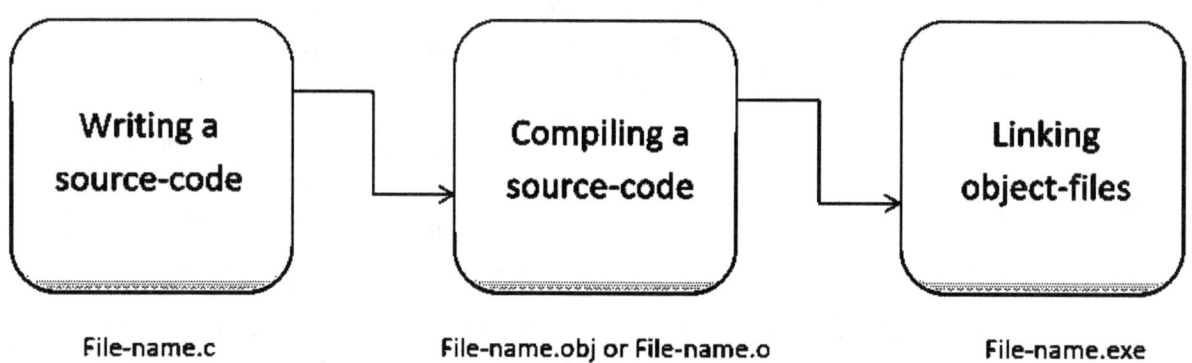

Various compilers are available online. You can use any of those compilers. Most of the compilers can execute both 'C' and 'C++' programs. There are some popular compilers available online. They are as follows:

- Turbo C
- Clang compiler
- Portable 'C' compiler
- MinGW compiler (Minimalist GNU for Windows)

CHAPTER-6: Hello World Program in C

```c
#include <stdio.h>

int main()
{
    printf("hello, world\n");
}
```

Hello World Program in C using Functions

```c
#include
void hello(){
    printf("Hello World");
}
int main()
{
   //Calling a function here
   hello();
   return 0;
}
```

CHAPTER-7: Printing Number Entered by User

```c
#include <stdio.h>
int main()
{
   int num;
   /* The printf() functions is used for displaying
    * the message or output on the screen. Here we
    * are displaying a message for the user.
    *
    */
   printf("Enter an integer: ");

   /* Here scanf() function reads the integer value
    * entered by user and stores it into the variable
    * num
    */
   scanf("%d", &num);

   // displaying the value of num using printf
   printf("The number entered by user is: %d", num);
   return 0;
}
```

CHAPTER-8: Adding Two Numbers

```c
#include<stdio.h>

int main() {
    int a, b, sum;

    printf("\nEnter two no: ");
    scanf("%d %d", &a, &b);

    sum = a + b;

    printf("Sum : %d", sum);

    return(0);
}
```

CHAPTER-9: Finding Quotient and Remainder

```c
#include<stdio.h>
#include<conio.h>
void main()
{
    int a, b, q, r;
    printf("Enter the dividend: ");
    scanf("%d", &a);
    printf("Enter the divisor: ");
    scanf("%d", &b);
    q=a/b;
    r=a%b;
    printf("\nThe value of quotient is: %d\n", q);
    printf("The value of remainder is: %d", r);
    getch();
}
```

CHAPTER-10: Finding Size of int, float, double and char in Your System

```c
#include<stdio.h>
int main()
{
    printf("Size of char: %ld byte\n",sizeof(char));
    printf("Size of int: %ld bytes\n",sizeof(int));
    printf("Size of float: %ld bytes\n",sizeof(float));
    printf("Size of double: %ld bytes", sizeof(double));
    return 0;
}
```

Output:

Size of char: 1 byte
Size of int: 4 bytes
Size of float: 4 bytes
Size of double: 8 bytes

CHAPTER-11: Swapping Two Numbers

```c
#include<stdio.h>
int main() {
    double first, second, temp;
    printf("Enter first number: ");
    scanf("%lf", &first);
    printf("Enter second number: ");
    scanf("%lf", &second);

    // Value of first is assigned to temp
    temp = first;

    // Value of second is assigned to first
    first = second;

    // Value of temp (initial value of first) is assigned to second
    second = temp;

    // %.2lf displays number up to 2 decimal points
    printf("\nAfter swapping, firstNumber = %.2lf\n", first);
    printf("After swapping, secondNumber = %.2lf", second);
    return 0;
}
```

Output:

Enter first number: 1.20
Enter second number: 2.45

After swapping, firstNumber = 2.45
After swapping, secondNumber = 1.20

CHAPTER-12: Finding ASCII Value of a Character

```c
// C program to print
// ASCII Value of Character
#include <stdio.h>
int main()
{
    char c = 'P';

    // %d displays the integer value of a character
    // %c displays the actual character
    printf("The ASCII value of %c is %d", c, c);
    return 0;
}
```

Output:

The ASCII value of P is 80

CHAPTER-13: Multiplying two Numbers

```c
#include <stdio.h>
int main() {
    double a, b, product;
    printf("Enter two numbers: ");
    scanf("%lf %lf", &a, &b);

    // Calculating product
    product = a * b;

    // %.2lf displays number up to 2 decimal point
    printf("Product = %.2lf", product);

    return 0;
}
```

Output:

Enter two numbers: 3.1

2.11

Product = 6.54

CHAPTER-14: Finding Area and Circumference of Circle

```
#include<stdio.h>
int main() {
    float radius, area;
    printf("\nEnter the radius of Circle : ");
    scanf("%d", &radius);
    area = 3.14 * radius * radius;
    printf("\nArea of Circle : %f", area);
    return (0);
}
```

Output:

Enter radius of a circle : 1
Area of circle : 3.14
Circumference : 6.28

CHAPTER-15: Converting a person's name in Abbreviated

```c
#include<stdio.h>
int main()
{
    char fname[20], mname[20], lname[20];
    printf("Enter The First Name Middle Name & Last Name \n");
    scanf("%s %s %s", fname, mname, lname);
    printf("Abbreviated name: ");
    printf("%c. %c. %s\n", fname[0], mname[0], lname);
    return 0;


}
```

CHAPTER-16: Calculating A Simple Interest

```
#include<stdio.h>
int main()
{
int p,r,t,int_amt;
printf("Input principle, Rate of interest & time to find simple interest: \n");
scanf("%d%d%d",&p,&r,&t);
int_amt=(p*r*t)/100;
printf("Simple interest = %d",int_amt);
return 0;
}
```

Output

Input Data: p = 10000, r = 10%, t = 12 year

Input principle, Rate of interest & time to find simple interest:

Simple interest = 12000

CHAPTER-17: Finding the Largest Number Among Three Numbers

```c
#include <stdio.h>
int main() {
    double n1, n2, n3;
    printf("Enter three different numbers: ");
    scanf("%lf %lf %lf", &n1, &n2, &n3);

    // if n1 is greater than both n2 and n3, n1 is the largest
    if (n1 >= n2 && n1 >= n3)
        printf("%.2f is the largest number.", n1);

    // if n2 is greater than both n1 and n3, n2 is the largest
    if (n2 >= n1 && n2 >= n3)
        printf("%.2f is the largest number.", n2);

    // if n3 is greater than both n1 and n2, n3 is the largest
    if (n3 >= n1 && n3 >= n2)
        printf("%.2f is the largest number.", n3);

    return 0;
}
```

Output

Enter three numbers: -4.5

3.9

5.6

5.60 is the largest number.

CHAPTER-18: Finding The Gross Salary of an Employee

```c
#include<stdio.h>

int main() {
    int gross_salary, basic, da, ta;

    printf("Enter basic salary : ");
    scanf("%d", &basic);

    da = (10 * basic) / 100;
    ta = (12 * basic) / 100;

    gross_salary = basic + da + ta;

    printf("\nGross salary : %d", gross_salary);
    return (0);
}
```

Output

Enter basic Salary: 1000

Gross Salary: 1220

CHAPTER-19: Calculating Percentage of 5 Subjects

```c
#include<stdio.h>
#include<conio.h>
void main()
{
    int s1,s2,s3,s4,s5,total=500,sum=0;
    float per;
    clrscr();
    printf("Enter Marks of 5 Subjects: ");
    scanf("%d%d%d%d%d",&s1,&s2,&s3,&s4,&s5);
    sum=s1+s2+s3+s4+s5;
    printf("Sum of 5 Subjects is: %d\n",sum);
    per=(sum*100)/total;
    printf("Percentage is: %f",per);
    getch();
}
```

Output

Enter Marks of 5 Subjects: 80 70 85 83 90
Sum of 5 Subjects is: 408
Percentage is: 81.000000

CHAPTER-20: Converting Temperature Celsius into Fahrenheit

```c
#include <stdio.h>

int main()
{
    float celsius, fahrenheit;

    /* Input temperature in celsius */
    printf("Enter temperature in Celsius: ");
    scanf("%f", &celsius);

    /* celsius to fahrenheit conversion formula */
    fahrenheit = (celsius * 9 / 5) + 32;

    printf("%.2f Celsius = %.2f Fahrenheit", celsius, fahrenheit);

    return 0;
}
```

Output

Enter temperature in Celsius: 100
100 Celsius = 212.00 Fahrenheit

CHAPTER-21: Finding out the size of the different data types in C

```
#include <stdio.h>
#include <conio.h>
main()
{
    clrscr();
    printf("short int is %2d bytes \n", sizeof(short int));
    printf("int is %2d bytes \n", sizeof(int));
    printf("int * is %2d bytes \n", sizeof(int *));
    printf("long int is %2d bytes \n", sizeof(long int));
    printf("long int * is %2d bytes \n", sizeof(long int *));
    printf("signed int is %2d bytes \n", sizeof(signed int));
    printf("unsigned int is %2d bytes \n", sizeof(unsigned int));
    printf("\n");
    printf("float is %2d bytes \n", sizeof(float));
    printf("float * is %2d bytes \n", sizeof(float *));
    printf("double is %2d bytes \n", sizeof(double));
    printf("double * is %2d bytes \n", sizeof(double *));
    printf("long double is %2d bytes \n", sizeof(long double));
    printf("\n");
    printf("signed char is %2d bytes \n", sizeof(signed char));
    printf("char is %2d bytes \n", sizeof(char));
```

```
        printf("char * is %2d bytes \n", sizeof(char *));
        printf("unsigned char is %2d bytes \n", sizeof(unsigned char));
        getch();
}
```

CHAPTER-22: Checking Whether a Number is Positive or Negative

```
#include <stdio.h>
void main()
{
    int num;

    printf("Input a number :");
    scanf("%d", &num);
    if (num >= 0)
        printf("%d is a positive number \n", num);
    else
        printf("%d is a negative number \n", num);
}
```

Output:

Input a number :15
15 is a positive number

CHAPTER-23: Checking whether a character is a vowel or not

```c
#include <stdio.h>
int main()
{
  char ch;

  printf("Enter a character\n");
  scanf("%c", &ch);

  // Checking both lower and upper case, || is the OR operator

  if (ch == 'a' || ch == 'A' || ch == 'e' || ch == 'E' || ch == 'i' || ch == 'I' || ch =='o' || ch=='O' || ch == 'u' || ch == 'U')
    printf("%c is a vowel.\n", ch);
  else
    printf("%c isn't a vowel.\n", ch);

  return 0;
}
```

Output:

Enter a character

```
G
G isn't a vowel.
```

CHAPTER-24: Calculating Factorial of a Number

```c
#include <stdio.h>
int main() {
    int n, i;
    unsigned long long fact = 1;
    printf("Enter an integer: ");
    scanf("%d", &n);

    // displays an error if the user enters a negative integer
    if (n < 0)
        printf("Error! Factorial of a negative number doesn't exist.");
    else {
        for (i = 1; i <= n; ++i) {
            fact *= i;
        }
        printf("Factorial of %d = %llu", n, fact);
    }

    return 0;
}
```

Output:

```
Enter an integer: 10
Factorial of 10 = 3628800
```

CHAPTER-25: Reading Integer (N) and Printing First Three Powers (N^1,N^2,N^3)

```c
#include<stdio.h>
#include<math.h>
int main()
{
  int num;
  printf("\nEnter The Number .\n");
  scanf("%d",&num);
  printf("\nOutput Is\n\n");
  printf("%d   ,%d   ,%d \n\n",num,num*num,num*num*num);
  return 0;
}
```

CHAPTER-26: Swapping two numbers without third variable

```c
#include<stdio.h>
 int main()
{
int a=10, b=20;
printf("Before swap a=%d b=%d",a,b);
a=a+b;//a=30 (10+20)
b=a-b;//b=10 (30-20)
a=a-b;//a=20 (30-10)
printf("\nAfter swap a=%d b=%d",a,b);
return 0;
}
```

Output:

Before swap a=10 b=20
After swap a=20 b=10

CHAPTER-27: Printing Address of Variable

```c
#include <stdio.h>

int main(void)
{
    // declare variables
    int a;
    float b;
    char c;

    printf("Address of a: %p\n", &a);
    printf("Address of b: %p\n", &b);
    printf("Address of c: %p\n", &c);

    return 0;
}
```

Output:

```
Address of a: 0x7ffd3d518618
Address of b: 0x7ffd3d51861c
Address of c: 0x7ffd3d518617
```

CHAPTER-28: Checking Whether a Number is Even or Odd

```c
#include <stdio.h>
int main() {
    int num;
    printf("Enter an integer: ");
    scanf("%d", &num);

    (num % 2 == 0) ? printf("%d is even.", num) : printf("%d is odd.", num);
    return 0;
}
```

Output:

Enter an integer: 33
33 is odd.

CHAPTER-29: Checking whether an Alphabet is Vowel or Consonant

```c
#include <stdio.h>
int main()
{
    char ch;
    bool isVowel = false;

    printf("Enter an alphabet: ");
    scanf("%c",&ch);

    if(ch=='a'||ch=='A'||ch=='e'||ch=='E'||ch=='i'||ch=='I'
         ||ch=='o'||ch=='O'||ch=='u'||ch=='U')
    {
     isVowel = true;

    }
    if (isVowel == true)
        printf("%c is a Vowel", ch);
    else
        printf("%c is a Consonant", ch);
    return 0;
}
```

Output:

Enter an alphabet: E

E is a Vowel

CHAPTER-30: Finding the Largest Number Among Three Numbers

```c
#include <stdio.h>
int main() {
    double n1, n2, n3;
    printf("Enter three numbers: ");
    scanf("%lf %lf %lf", &n1, &n2, &n3);

    // if n1 is greater than both n2 and n3, n1 is the largest
    if (n1 >= n2 && n1 >= n3)
        printf("%.2lf is the largest number.", n1);

    // if n2 is greater than both n1 and n3, n2 is the largest
    else if (n2 >= n1 && n2 >= n3)
        printf("%.2lf is the largest number.", n2);

    // if both above conditions are false, n3 is the largest
    else
        printf("%.2lf is the largest number.", n3);

    return 0;
}
```

Output:

Enter three numbers: -4.5

3.9

5.6

5.60 is the largest number.

CHAPTER-31: FINDING THE ROOTS OF A QUADRATIC EQUATION

```c
#include <math.h>
#include <stdio.h>
int main() {
    double a, b, c, discriminant, root1, root2, realPart, imagPart;
    printf("Enter coefficients a, b and c: ");
    scanf("%lf %lf %lf", &a, &b, &c);

    discriminant = b * b - 4 * a * c;

    // condition for real and different roots
    if (discriminant > 0) {
        root1 = (-b + sqrt(discriminant)) / (2 * a);
        root2 = (-b - sqrt(discriminant)) / (2 * a);
        printf("root1 = %.2lf and root2 = %.2lf", root1, root2);
    }

    // condition for real and equal roots
    else if (discriminant == 0) {
        root1 = root2 = -b / (2 * a);
        printf("root1 = root2 = %.2lf;", root1);
    }

    // if roots are not real
```

```c
    else {
        realPart = -b / (2 * a);
        imagPart = sqrt(-discriminant) / (2 * a);
        printf("root1 = %.2lf+%.2lfi and root2 = %.2f-%.2fi",
realPart, imagPart, realPart, imagPart);
    }


    return 0;
}
```

Output:

Enter three numbers: -4.5

Enter coefficients a, b and c: 2.3

4

5.6

root1 = -0.87+1.30i and root2 = -0.87-1.30i

CHAPTER-32: Calculating the Sum of Natural Numbers

```c
#include <stdio.h>
int main() {
    int n, i, sum = 0;
    printf("Enter a positive integer: ");
    scanf("%d", &n);
    i = 1;

    while (i <= n) {
        sum += i;
        ++i;
    }

    printf("Sum = %d", sum);
    return 0;
}
```

Output:

Enter a positive integer: 100

Sum = 5050

CHAPTER-33: Checking Leap Year

```c
#include <stdio.h>
int main() {
    int year;
    printf("Enter a year: ");
    scanf("%d", &year);

    // leap year if perfectly divisible by 400
    if (year % 400 == 0) {
        printf("%d is a leap year.", year);
    }
    // not a leap year if divisible by 100
    // but not divisible by 400
    else if (year % 100 == 0) {
        printf("%d is not a leap year.", year);
    }
    // leap year if not divisible by 100
    // but divisible by 4
    else if (year % 4 == 0) {
        printf("%d is a leap year.", year);
    }
    // all other years are not leap years
    else {
        printf("%d is not a leap year.", year);
    }

    return 0;
```

}

Output:

Enter a year: 2012

2012 is a leap year.

CHAPTER-34: Factorial Program using recursion in C

```c
#include<stdio.h>

long factorial(int n)
{
  if (n == 0)
    return 1;
  else
    return(n * factorial(n-1));
}

void main()
{
  int number;
  long fact;
  printf("Enter a number: ");
  scanf("%d", &number);

  fact = factorial(number);
  printf("Factorial of %d is %ld\n", number, fact);
  return 0;
}
```

Output:

Enter a number: 6
Factorial of 5 is: 720

CHAPTER-35: Generating Multiplication Table

```c
#include <stdio.h>
int main() {
  int n, i;
  printf("Enter an integer: ");
  scanf("%d", &n);
  for (i = 1; i <= 10; ++i) {
    printf("%d * %d = %d \n", n, i, n * i);
  }
  return 0;
}
```

Output:

Enter an integer: 9

9 * 1 = 9

9 * 2 = 18

9 * 3 = 27

9 * 4 = 36

9 * 5 = 45

9 * 6 = 54

9 * 7 = 63

9 * 8 = 72

9 * 9 = 81

9 * 10 = 90

CHAPTER-36: Fibonacci Series using recursion in C

```c
#include<stdio.h>
void printFibonacci(int n){
    static int n1=0,n2=1,n3;
    if(n>0){
        n3 = n1 + n2;
        n1 = n2;
        n2 = n3;
        printf("%d ",n3);
        printFibonacci(n-1);
    }
}
int main(){
    int n;
    printf("Enter the number of elements: ");
    scanf("%d",&n);
    printf("Fibonacci Series: ");
    printf("%d %d ",0,1);
    printFibonacci(n-2);//n-2 because 2 numbers are already printed
    return 0;
}
```

Output:

Enter the number of elements:15

0 1 1 2 3 5 8 13 21 34 55 89 144 233 377

CHAPTER-37: Finding GCD of two Numbers

```c
#include <stdio.h>
int main()
{
    int n1, n2;

    printf("Enter two positive integers: ");
    scanf("%d %d",&n1,&n2);

    while(n1!=n2)
    {
        if(n1 > n2)
            n1 -= n2;
        else
            n2 -= n1;
    }
    printf("GCD = %d",n1);

    return 0;
}
```

Output:
Enter two positive integers: 81
153
GCD = 9

CHAPTER-38: Finding LCM of two Numbers

```c
#include <stdio.h>
int main() {
    int n1, n2, i, gcd, lcm;
    printf("Enter two positive integers: ");
    scanf("%d %d", &n1, &n2);

    for (i = 1; i <= n1 && i <= n2; ++i) {

        // check if i is a factor of both integers
        if (n1 % i == 0 && n2 % i == 0)
            gcd = i;
    }

    lcm = (n1 * n2) / gcd;

    printf("The LCM of two numbers %d and %d is %d.", n1, n2, lcm);
    return 0;
}
```

Output:
Enter two positive integers: 72
120
The LCM of two numbers 72 and 120 is 360.

CHAPTER-39: Reversing a Number

```c
#include <stdio.h>
int main() {
    int n, rev = 0, remainder;
    printf("Enter an integer: ");
    scanf("%d", &n);
    while (n != 0) {
        remainder = n % 10;
        rev = rev * 10 + remainder;
        n /= 10;
    }
    printf("Reversed number = %d", rev);
    return 0;
}
```

Output:

Enter an integer: 345

Reversed number = 543

CHAPTER-40: Calculating the Power of a Number

```c
#include <stdio.h>
int main() {
    int base, exp;
    long double result = 1.0;
    printf("Enter a base number: ");
    scanf("%d", &base);
    printf("Enter an exponent: ");
    scanf("%d", &exp);

    while (exp != 0) {
        result *= base;
        --exp;
    }
    printf("Answer = %.0Lf", result);
    return 0;
}
```

Output:

Enter a base number: 2

Enter an exponent: 4

Answer = 16

CHAPTER-41: Checking Whether a Number is Palindrome or Not

```c
#include <stdio.h>
int main() {
  int n, reversed = 0, remainder, original;
    printf("Enter an integer: ");
    scanf("%d", &n);
    original = n;

    // reversed integer is stored in reversed variable
    while (n != 0) {
        remainder = n % 10;
        reversed = reversed * 10 + remainder;
        n /= 10;
    }


    // palindrome if orignal and reversed are equal
    if (original == reversed)
        printf("%d is a palindrome.", original);
    else
        printf("%d is not a palindrome.", original);

    return 0;
}
```

Output:

Enter an integer: 151

151 is a palindrome.

CHAPTER-42: Checking Whether a Number is Prime or Not

```c
#include<stdio.h>
int main(){
int n,i,m=0,flag=0;
printf("Enter the number to check prime:");
scanf("%d",&n);
m=n/2;
for(i=2;i<=m;i++)
{
if(n%i==0)
{
printf("Number is not prime");
flag=1;
break;
}
}
if(flag==0)
printf("Number is prime");
return 0;
 }
```

Output:

Enter the number to check prime:29
Number is prime

CHAPTER-43: Displaying Prime Numbers Between Two Intervals

```c
#include <stdio.h>

int main() {
    int low, high, i, flag;
    printf("Enter two numbers(intervals): ");
    scanf("%d %d", &low, &high);
    printf("Prime numbers between %d and %d are: ", low, high);

    // iteration until low is not equal to high
    while (low < high) {
        flag = 0;

        // ignore numbers less than 2
        if (low <= 1) {
            ++low;
            continue;
        }

        // if low is a non-prime number, flag will be 1
        for (i = 2; i <= low / 2; ++i) {

            if (low % i == 0) {
                flag = 1;
                break;
            }
        }
```

```
        if (flag == 0)
            printf("%d ", low);


        // to check prime for the next number
        // increase low by 1
        ++low;
    }


    return 0;
}
```

Output:

Enter two numbers(intervals): 20
50
Prime numbers between 20 and 50 are: 23 29 31 37 41 43 47

CHAPTER-44: Checking Armstrong Number

```c
#include<stdio.h>
 int main()
{
int n,r,sum=0,temp;
printf("enter the number=");
scanf("%d",&n);
temp=n;
while(n>0)
{
r=n%10;
sum=sum+(r*r*r);
n=n/10;
}
if(temp==sum)
printf("armstrong  number ");
else
printf("not armstrong number");
return 0;
}
```

Output:
enter the number=5
not armstrong number

CHAPTER-45: Displaying Armstrong Number Between Two Intervals

```c
// C program to print the Armstrong numbers between the two intervals

#include <stdio.h>
#include <math.h>

int main()
{
int start, end, i, temp1, temp2, remainder, n = 0, result = 0;

printf("Enter start value and end value : ");
scanf("%d %d", &start, &end);
printf("\nArmstrong numbers between %d an %d are: ", start, end);

for(i = start + 1; i < end; ++i)
{
temp2 = i;
temp1 = i;

while (temp1 != 0)
{
temp1 /= 10;
++n;
}
```

```c
while (temp2 != 0)
{
remainder = temp2 % 10;
result += pow(remainder, n);
temp2 /= 10;
}

if (result == i) {
printf("%d ", i);
}

n = 0;
result = 0;

}
printf("\n");
return 0;
}
```

Output:

Enter start value and end value: 100 500
Armstrong numbers between 100 and 500 are:370 371 407

CHAPTER-46: Finding Factors of a Number

```c
#include<stdio.h>

int main()
{
    int num, count = 1;

    printf("Enter a number\n");
    scanf("%d", &num);

    printf("Factors of %d are:\n", num);

    while(count <= num)
    {
        if(num % count == 0)
        {
            printf("%d\n", count);
        }
        count++;
    }

    return 0;
}
```

Output:

Enter a number

50

Factors of 50 are:

1
2
5
10
25
50

CHAPTER-47: Making a Simple Calculator to Add, Subtract, Multiply or Divide Using switch…case

```c
#include <stdio.h>
int main() {
  char op;
  double first, second;
  printf("Enter an operator (+, -, *, /): ");
  scanf("%c", &op);
  printf("Enter two operands: ");
  scanf("%lf %lf", &first, &second);

  switch (op) {
    case '+':
      printf("%.1lf + %.1lf = %.1lf", first, second, first + second);
      break;
    case '-':
      printf("%.1lf - %.1lf = %.1lf", first, second, first - second);
      break;
    case '*':
      printf("%.1lf * %.1lf = %.1lf", first, second, first * second);
      break;
    case '/':
      printf("%.1lf / %.1lf = %.1lf", first, second, first / second);
      break;
    // operator doesn't match any case constant
    default:
```

```c
            printf("Error! operator is not correct");
    }


    return 0;
}
```

Output:

Enter an operator (+, -, *,): *

Enter two operands: 1.5

4.5

1.5 * 4.5 = 6.8

CHAPTER-48: Printing A Message Multiple Times Using Loop

```c
#include <stdio.h>
int main(){
    char name[50],i;
    printf("\nEnter your name :");
    scanf("%s",name);
    for(i=0;i<10;i++){
        printf("%s\n",name);
    }
    return 0;
}
```

Output:

Enter your name :Tt

Tt

Tt

Tt

Tt

Tt

CHAPTER-49: Printing Truth Table of XY+Z Using Loop

```c
#include<stdio.h>
#include<conio.h>

void main()
{
int x,y,z;
clrscr(); //to clear the screen
printf("XtYtZtXY+Z");

for(x=0;x<=1;++x)
for(y=0;y<=1;++y)
for(z=0;z<=1;++z)
{
if(x*y+z==2)
printf("nn%dt%dt%dt1",x,y,z);
else
printf("nn%dt%dt%dt%d",x,y,z,x*y+z);
}
getch(); //to stop the screen
}
```

Output:

X Y Z XY+Z

0 0 0 0

0 0 1 1

0 1 0 0

0 1 1 1

1 0 0 0

1 0 1 1

1 1 0 1

1 1 1 1

CHAPTER-50: Converting Decimal Number to Binary Number Using Loop

```c
#include <stdio.h>
#include <math.h>

long decimalToBinary(int decimalnum)
{
    long binarynum = 0;
    int rem, temp = 1;

    while (decimalnum!=0)
    {
        rem = decimalnum%2;
        decimalnum = decimalnum / 2;
        binarynum = binarynum + rem*temp;
        temp = temp * 10;
    }
    return binarynum;
}

int main()
{
    int decimalnum;
    printf("Enter a Decimal Number: ");
    scanf("%d", &decimalnum);
    printf("Equivalent Binary Number is: %ld", decimalToBinary(decimalnum));
    return 0;
}
```

Output:

Enter a Decimal Number: 234

Equivalent Binary Number is: 11101010

CHAPTER-51: Swapping Two Numbers Using Functions

```c
#include<stdio.h>
void swap(int *,int *);
int main()
{
    int n1,n2;
    printf("Input 1st number : ");
    scanf("%d",&n1);
    printf("Input 2nd number : ");
    scanf("%d",&n2);

    printf("Before swapping: n1 = %d, n2 = %d ",n1,n2);
     //pass the address of both variables to the function.
    swap(&n1,&n2);

    printf("\nAfter swapping: n1 = %d, n2 = %d \n\n",n1,n2);
    return 0;
}

void swap(int *p,int *q)
{
    int tmp;
    tmp = *p; // tmp store the value of n1
    *p=*q;    // *p store the value of *q that is value of n2
    *q=tmp;   // *q store the value of tmp that is the value of n1
}
```

Output:

Input 1st number : 2
Input 2nd number : 4
Before swapping: n1 = 2, n2 = 4
After swapping: n1 = 4, n2 = 2

CHAPTER-52: Checking Prime Number by Creating a Function

```c
#include<stdio.h>
int checkPrime(int number)
{
  int count = 0;

  for(int i=2; i<=number/2; i++)
  {
    if(number%i == 0)
    {
      count=1;
      break;
    }
  }

  if(number == 1) count = 1;

  return count;
}

int main()
{
  int number ;

  printf("Enter number: ");
  scanf("%d",&number);

  if(checkPrime(number) == 0)
```

```c
        printf("%d is a prime number.", number);
    else
        printf("%d is not a prime number.", number);

    return 0;
}
```

Output:

```
Enter number: 17
17 is a prime number.
```

CHAPTER-53: Calculating Factorial of a Number Using Recursion

```c
#include<stdio.h>
long int multiplyNumbers(int n);
int main() {
    int n;
    printf("Enter a positive integer: ");
    scanf("%d",&n);
    printf("Factorial of %d = %ld", n, multiplyNumbers(n));
    return 0;
}

long int multiplyNumbers(int n) {
    if (n>=1)
        return n*multiplyNumbers(n-1);
    else
        return 1;
}
```

Output:

Enter a positive integer: 5
Factorial of 5 = 120

CHAPTER-54: Finding Fibonacci Series Using Functions

```c
#include<stdio.h>
void fibonacciSeries(int range)
{
    int a=0, b=1, c;
    while (a<=range)
    {
      printf("%d\t", a);
      c = a+b;
      a = b;
      b = c;
    }
}

int main()
{
    int range;

    printf("Enter range: ");
    scanf("%d", &range);

    printf("The fibonacci series is: \n");

    fibonacciSeries(range);

    return 0;
}
```

Output:

Enter the term: 10
The fibonacci series is:
0 1 1 2 3 5 8 13 21 34

CHAPTER-55: Performing All Arithmetic Operations Using Functions

```c
#include <stdio.h>

// @function to make Addition
int Addition(int p, int q) {
    return p + q;
}

// @function to make Subtraction
int Subtraction(int p, int q) {
    return p - q;
}

// @function to make Multiplication
int Multiplication(int p, int q) {
    return p * q;
}

// @function to make Division
float Division(int p, int q) {
    return (float)p / q;
}

// @function to make Modulus
int Modulus(int p, int q) {
    return p % q;
}
```

```c
int main() {
    int p, q;

    // it will take two integer numbers
    printf("Enter any two positive integer numbers:\n");
    scanf("%d%d", &p, &q);

    // It will call the all user-defined function
    // Then, print the final output of the program
    printf("\n");
    printf("Addition of       %d + %d = %d\n", p, q, Addition(p, q));
    printf("Subtraction of    %d - %d = %d\n", p, q, Subtraction(p, q));
    printf("Multiplication of %d * %d = %d\n", p, q, Multiplication(p, q));
    printf("Division of       %d / %d = %f\n", p, q, Division(p, q));
    printf("Modulus of        %d %% %d = %d\n", p, q, Modulus(p, q));

    return 0;
}
```

Output:

Enter any two positive integer numbers:
8
9

Addition of   8 + 9 = 17

```
Subtraction of     8 - 9 = -1
Multiplication of 8 * 9 = 72
Division of        8 / 9 = 0.888
Modulus of         8 % 9 = 8
```

CHAPTER-56: Calculating Power Using Recursion

```c
#include<stdio.h> // include stdio.h library
int power(int, int);

int main(void)
{
    int base, exponent;

    printf("Enter base: ");
    scanf("%d", &base);

    printf("Enter exponent: ");
    scanf("%d", &exponent);

    printf("%d^%d = %d", base, exponent, power(base, exponent));

    return 0; // return 0 to operating system
}

int power(int base, int exponent)
{

    //base condition
    if(exponent == 0)
    {
        return 1;
    }
```

```
    else
    {
        // recursive call
        return base * power(base, exponent - 1);
    }

}
```

Output:

```
Enter base: 5
Enter exponent: 5
5^5 = 3125
```

CHAPTER-57: Converting Binary Number to Decimal and vice-versa

```c
#include <stdio.h>
#include <conio.h>
void main()
{
    // declaration of variables
    int num, binary_num, decimal_num = 0, base = 1, rem;
    printf (" Enter a binary number with the combination of 0s and 1s \n");
    scanf (" %d", &num); // accept the binary number (0s and 1s)

    binary_num = num; // assign the binary number to the binary_num variable


    while ( num > 0)
    {
        rem = num % 10; /* divide the binary number by 10 and store the remainder in rem variable. */
        decimal_num = decimal_num + rem * base;
        num = num / 10; // divide the number with quotient
        base = base * 2;
    }


    printf ( " The binary number is %d \t", binary_num); // print the binary number
    printf (" \n The decimal number is %d \t", decimal_num); // print the decimal
```

```
    getch();
}
```
Output:

Enter a binary number with the combination of 0s and 1s
10111
 The binary number is 10111
 The decimal number is 23

CHAPTER-58: Converting Octal Number to Decimal and vice-versa

```c
#include <stdio.h>
#include <math.h>

int convertDecimalToOctal(int decimalNumber);
int main()
{
    int decimalNumber;

    printf("Enter a decimal number: ");
    scanf("%d", &decimalNumber);

    printf("%d in decimal = %d in octal", decimalNumber, convertDecimalToOctal(decimalNumber));

    return 0;
}

int convertDecimalToOctal(int decimalNumber)
{
    int octalNumber = 0, i = 1;

    while (decimalNumber != 0)
    {
        octalNumber += (decimalNumber % 8) * i;
        decimalNumber /= 8;
```

```
            i *= 10;
    }

    return octalNumber;
}
```

Output:

```
Enter a decimal number: 67
67 in decimal = 103 in octal
```

CHAPTER-59: Converting Binary Number to Octal and vice-versa

```c
#include <stdio.h>
#include <math.h>
int binary_octal(int n);
int octal_binary(int n);
int main()
{
    int n;
    char c;
    printf("Instructions:\n");
    printf("1. Enter alphabet 'o' to convert binary to octal.\n");
    printf("2. Enter alphabet 'b' to convert octal to binary.\n");
    scanf("%c",&c);
    if ( c=='o' || c=='O')
    {
        printf("Enter a binary number: ");
        scanf("%d",&n);
        printf("%d in binary = %d in octal", n, binary_octal(n));
    }
    if ( c=='b' || c=='B')
    {
        printf("Enter a octal number: ");
        scanf("%d",&n);
```

```c
        printf("%d in octal = %d in binary",n, octal_binary(n));
    }
    return 0;
}
int binary_octal(int n)   /* Function to convert binary to octal. */
{
    int octal=0, decimal=0, i=0;
    while(n!=0)
    {
        decimal+=(n%10)*pow(2,i);
        ++i;
        n/=10;
    }

/*At this point, the decimal variable contains corresponding decimal value of binary number. */

    i=1;
    while (decimal!=0)
    {
        octal+=(decimal%8)*i;
        decimal/=8;
        i*=10;
    }
    return octal;
}
int octal_binary(int n)   /* Function to convert octal to binary.*/
{
    int decimal=0, binary=0, i=0;
```

```
        while (n!=0)
        {
            decimal+=(n%10)*pow(8,i);
            ++i;
            n/=10;
        }
/* At this point, the decimal variable contains corresponding decimal value of that octal number. */
        i=1;
        while(decimal!=0)
        {
            binary+=(decimal%2)*i;
            decimal/=2;
            i*=10;
        }
        return binary;
}
```

Output:

Instructions:

1. Enter alphabet 'o' to convert binary to octal.

2. Enter alphabet 'b' convert octal to binary.

o

Enter a binary number: 10101

11011 in binary = 25 in octal

b

Enter an octal number: 16

16 in octal = 1110 in binary

CHAPTER-60: Converting A Lower Case To Upper Case using string

```c
#include<stdio.h>
#include<string.h>
int main()
{
    char s[100];

    // take input
    printf("Enter a string: ");
    scanf("%[^\n]",s);

    // display output
    printf("In Upper Case:\n");
    puts(strupr(s));

    return 0;
}
```

Output:

```
Enter a string: learn programming
In Upper Case:
LEARN PROGRAMMING
```

CHAPTER-61: Calculating Average of Numbers Using Arrays

```c
#include <stdio.h>

int main() {
    int array[10] = {1, 2, 3, 4, 5, 6, 7, 8, 9, 0};
    int sum, loop;
    float avg;

    sum = avg = 0;

    for(loop = 0; loop < 10; loop++) {
        sum = sum + array[loop];
    }

    avg = (float)sum / loop;
    printf("Average of array values is %.2f", avg);

    return 0;
}
```

Output:

Average of array values is 4.50

CHAPTER-62: Finding The Length Of Any String

```c
#include <stdio.h>
int main() {
    char s[] = "We learn Programming";
    int i;

    for (i = 0; s[i] != '\0'; ++i);

    printf("Length of the string: %d", i);
    return 0;
}
```

Output:

Length of the string: 20

CHAPTER-63: Checking Number Is Even Or Odd Using If/Else Statements

```c
#include <stdio.h>

int number;

void oddOrEven() {
  if (number % 2 == 0) {
    printf("%d is even.", number);
  } else {
    printf("%d is odd.", number);
  }
}

int main() {
  printf("Enter the value: ");
  scanf("%d", &number);
  oddOrEven();
  return 0;
}
```

Output:

Enter the value: 7
7 is odd.

CHAPTER-64: Checking Year Is Leap Year Or Not Using If/Else Statements

```c
#include <stdio.h>

int yr;
  printf ("Enter a year n");
  scanf ("%d", &yr);

  if (yr%4 == 0) {

     if(yr%100 == 0) {

        if(yr%400 == 0)
           printf("n It is LEAP YEAR.");
        else
           printf("n It is NOT LEAP YEAR.");
     }

     else {
          printf ("n It is LEAP YEAR.");
     }
  }
  else
     printf("n It is NOT LEAP YEAR.");
```

```
return 0;
}
```

Output:

```
Enter a year
2016
It is LEAP YEAR.
```

CHAPTER-65: Finding Max Number Among Given Three Number Using If/Else Statements

```c
/* C Program to find Largest of Three numbers using Else If
Statement */

#include <stdio.h>

int main()
{
 int a, b, c;

 printf("Please Enter three different values\n");
 scanf("%d %d %d", &a, &b, &c);

 if (a > b && a > c)
  {
   printf("\n%d is Greater Than both %d and %d", a, b, c);
  }
 else if (b > a && b > c)
  {
   printf("\n%d is Greater Than both %d and %d", b, a, c);
  }
 else if (c > a && c > b)
  {
```

```
    printf("\n%d is Greater Than both %d and %d", c, a, b);
  }
 else
  {
    printf("\nEither any two values or all the three values are equal");
  }
 return 0;
}
```

Output:

```
Please Enter three different values
10
3
7


10 is Greater Than both 3 and 7
```

CHAPTER-66: Finding Quotient And Reminder Of Two Numbers Using If/Else Statements

```c
// C program to find quotient
// and remainder of two numbers

#include <stdio.h>

int main()
{
    int A, B, quotient = 0, remainder = 0;

    // Ask user to enter the two numbers
    printf("Enter two numbers A and B : \n");

    // Read two numbers from the user || A = 17, B = 5
    scanf("%d%d", &A, &B);

    // Calclulate the quotient of A and B using '/' operator
    quotient = A / B;

    // Calclulate the remainder of A and B using '%' operator
    remainder = A % B;
```

```c
    // Print the result
    printf("Quotient when A/B is: %d\n", quotient);
    printf("Remainder when A/B is: %d", remainder);

    return 0;
}
```

Output:

```
Enter two numbers A and B : 19 7
Quotient when A/B is: 2
Remainder when A/B is: 5
```

CHAPTER-67: Temperature Conversion Celsius To Fahrenheit And Vice Versa Using Switch Case

```c
/* C Program to convert temperature from Fahrenheit to Celsius
and vice versa.*/

#include <stdio.h>

int main()
{

    float fh,cl;
    int choice;

    printf("\n1: Convert temperature from Fahrenheit to Celsius.");
    printf("\n2: Convert temperature from Celsius to Fahrenheit.");
    printf("\nEnter your choice (1, 2): ");
    scanf("%d",&choice);

    if(choice ==1){
        printf("\nEnter temperature in Fahrenheit: ");
        scanf("%f",&fh);
        cl= (fh - 32) / 1.8;
```

```
        printf("Temperature in Celsius: %.2f",cl);
    }
    else if(choice==2){
        printf("\nEnter temperature in Celsius: ");
        scanf("%f",&cl);
        fh= (cl*1.8)+32;
        printf("Temperature in Fahrenheit: %.2f",fh);
    }
    else{
        printf("\nIt's not a valid Choice!");
    }
    return 0;
}
```

Output:

First Run:

1: Convert temperature from Fahrenheit to Celsius.

2: Convert temperature from Celsius to Fahrenheit.

Enter your choice (1, 2): 1

Enter temperature in Fahrenheit: 97.5

Temperature in Celsius: 36.38

Second Run:

1: Convert temperature from Fahrenheit to Celsius.

2: Convert temperature from Celsius to Fahrenheit.

Enter your choice (1, 2): 2

Enter temperature in Celsius: 36.38

Temperature in Fahrenheit: 97.50

Third Run:

1: Convert temperature from Fahrenheit to Celsius.

2: Convert temperature from Celsius to Fahrenheit.

Enter your choice (1, 2): 3

It's not a valid Choice!

CHAPTER-68: Calculating Area Of Circle Rectangle And Triangle Using Switch Case

```c
#include<stdio.h>

#define PI 3.147

void main()
{
    float radius, length, breadth;
    float base, height, area;
    int choice;

    printf("Enter\n");
    printf("1. To find area of triangle\n2. To find area of Square\n");
    printf("3. To find area of circle\n4. To find area of rectangle\n");

    scanf("%d",&choice);
    switch(choice)
    {
        case 1:
            printf("Enter base and height of a triangle\n");
```

```c
        scanf("%f %f", &base, &height);

        area = (1.0/2) * base * height;

        printf("Area of Triangle:\t%f\n", area);

        break;

    case 2:
        printf("Enter length of a Square\n");
        scanf("%f", &length);

        area = length * length;

        printf("Area of Square:\t%f\n", area);

        break;

    case 3:
        printf("Enter the radius of a Circle\n");
        scanf("%f", &radius);

        area = PI * radius * radius;

        printf("Area of Circle:\t%f\n", area);

        break;

    case 4:
        printf("Enter the length and breadth of a Rectangle\n");
```

```c
            scanf("%f %f", &length, &breadth);

            area = length * breadth;

            printf("Area of Rectangle:\t%f\n", area);

            break;

        default:
            printf("It's not a valid Choice\n");
    }
}
```

Output:

Output 1

Enter

1. To find area of triangle

2. To find area of square

3. To find area of circle

4. To find area of rectangle

1

Enter base & height of a triangle

4

5

Area of Triangle: 10.000000

Output 2

Enter

1. To find area of triangle

2. To find area of square

3. To find area of circle

4. To find area of rectangle

2

Enter length of a square

4

Area of Square: 16.000000

Output 3

Enter

1. To find area of triangle

2. To find area of Square

3. To find area of circle

4. To find area of rectangle

3

Enter the radius of a Circle

5

Area of Circle: 78.675003

Output 4

Enter

1. To find area of triangle

2. To find area of Square

3. To find area of circle

4. To find area of rectangle

4

Enter the length and breadth of a Rectangle

```
7
8
Area of Rectangle:   56.000000
```

CHAPTER-69: Reading Infinite Number Then Arrange Ascending Order Using Pointer

```c
#include<stdio.h>
#include<stdlib.h>

int main()
{
 int *p,*q,i=1,j,k,temp;    //q for storing address of 1st number
 printf("Enter infinite Numbers(-1 to stop reading) :: \n");

 printf("\nEnter %d Number :: ",i);
 p=(int*)malloc(sizeof(int));
 scanf("%d",&p[0]);

 while(p[i-1]!=-1) //read until -1 is entered
 {
  i++;

  p=(int*)realloc(p,sizeof(int)*i);
  q=p;
  printf("\nEnter %d Number :: ",i);
```

```c
    scanf("%d",&p[i-1]);
}


p=q;


//sorting numbers using bubble sort
for(j=1;j<i;++j)
{
 for(k=0;k<i-j-1;++k)
 {
  if(p[k]>p[k+1])
  {
   temp=p[k];
   p[k]=p[k+1];
   p[k+1]=temp;
  }
 }
}

printf("\n");

printf("\nAfter Sorting, Numbers are :: ");
for(j=0;j<i-1;++j)
{
 printf(" %d",p[j]);
}

printf("\n");

return 0;
}
```

Output:

Enter infinite Numbers(-1 to stop reading) ::

Enter 1 Number :: 3

Enter 2 Number :: 1

Enter 3 Number :: 5

Enter 4 Number :: 2

Enter 5 Number :: 4

Enter 6 Number :: 7

Enter 7 Number :: 6

Enter 8 Number :: 9

Enter 9 Number :: 8

Enter 10 Number :: 0

Enter 11 Number :: -1

After Sorting, Numbers are ::   0 1 2 3 4 5 6 7 8 9

CHAPTER-70: Storing Information of a Student in a Structure

```c
#include<stdio.h>
struct student
{
    char name[50];
    int roll;
    float marks;
} s[10];

int main()
{
    int i;

    printf("Enter information of students:\n");

    // storing information
    for(i=0; i<10; ++i)
    {
        s[i].roll = i+1;
```

```c
        printf("\nFor roll number%d,\n",s[i].roll);

        printf("Enter name: ");
        scanf("%s",s[i].name);

        printf("Enter marks: ");
        scanf("%f",&s[i].marks);

        printf("\n");
    }

    printf("Displaying Information:\n\n");
    // displaying information
    for(i=0; i<10; ++i)
    {
        printf("\nRoll number: %d\n",i+1);
        printf("Name: ");
        puts(s[i].name);
        printf("Marks: %.1f",s[i].marks);
        printf("\n");
    }
    return 0;
}
```

Output:

Enter information of students:

For roll number1,
Enter name: Andrew
Enter marks: 94

For roll number2,

Enter name: David

Enter marks: 83

.

.

.

Displaying Information:

Roll number: 1

Name: Andrew

Marks: 94

CHAPTER-71: Calculating Difference Between Two Time Period

```c
#include
struct TIME
{
  int seconds;
  int minutes;
  int hours;
};
void differenceBetweenTimePeriod(struct TIME t1, struct TIME t2, struct TIME *diff);

int main()
{
    struct TIME startTime, stopTime, diff;

    printf("Enter start time: \n");
    printf("Enter hours, minutes and seconds respectively: ");
    scanf("%d %d %d", &startTime.hours, &startTime.minutes, &startTime.seconds);
```

```c
    printf("Enter stop time: \n");
    printf("Enter hours, minutes and seconds respectively: ");
    scanf("%d %d %d", &stopTime.hours, &stopTime.minutes, &stopTime.seconds);


    // Calculate the difference between the start and stop time period.
    differenceBetweenTimePeriod(startTime, stopTime, &diff);


    printf("\nTIME DIFFERENCE: %d:%d:%d - ", startTime.hours, startTime.minutes, startTime.seconds);
    printf("%d:%d:%d  ", stopTime.hours, stopTime.minutes, stopTime.seconds);
    printf("=    %d:%d:%d\n", diff.hours, diff.minutes, diff.seconds);

    return 0;
}


void differenceBetweenTimePeriod(struct TIME start, struct TIME stop, struct TIME *diff)
{
    if(stop.seconds > start.seconds){
        --start.minutes;
        start.seconds += 60;
    }


    diff->seconds = start.seconds - stop.seconds;
    if(stop.minutes > start.minutes){
        --start.hours;
        start.minutes += 60;
    }
```

```
        diff->minutes = start.minutes - stop.minutes;
        diff->hours = start.hours - stop.hours;
}
```

Output:

Enter start time:
Enter hours, minutes and seconds respectively: 11
24
45
Enter stop time:
Enter hours, minutes and seconds respectively:6
10
11

TIME DIFFERENCE: 11:24:45 - 6:10:11 = 5:14:34